P9-AQY-466

How Far Is Far?
Comparing Geographical Distances

Vic Parker

Heinemann
LIBRARY
Chicago, Illinois

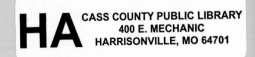
HA CASS COUNTY PUBLIC LIBRARY
400 E. MECHANIC
HARRISONVILLE, MO 64701

0 0022 04001875

www.heinemannraintree.com
Visit our website to find out more information about Heinemann-Raintree books.

To order:
☎ Phone 888-454-2279
🖥 Visit www.heinemannraintree.com to browse our catalog and order online.

© 2011 Heinemann Library
an imprint of Capstone Global Library, LLC
Chicago, Illinois

All rights reserved. No part of this publication may be reproduced or transmitted in any form or by any means, electronic or mechanical, including photocopying, recording, taping, or any information storage and retrieval system, without permission in writing from the publisher.

Edited by Nancy Dickmann, Rebecca Rissman, and Sian Smith
Designed by Victoria Allen
Picture research by Hannah Taylor
Original illustrations © Capstone Global Library 2011
Original illustrations by Victoria Allen
Production by Victoria Fitzgerald
Originated by Dot Gradations Ltd
Printed and bound in China by South China Printing Company Ltd

14 13 12 11 10
10 9 8 7 6 5 4 3 2 1

Library of Congress Cataloging-in-Publication Data
Parker, Victoria.
    How far is far?:comparing geographical distances / Vic Parker.
        p. cm.—(Measuring and comparing)
    Includes bibliographical references and index.
    ISBN 978-1-4329-3956-4 (hc)—ISBN 978-1-4329-3964-9 (pb) 1. Length measurement-Juvenile literature. 2. Map scales—Juvenile literature. 3. Distances-Measurement—Juvenile literature. I. Title.
    QC102.P366 2011
    912.01'4—dc   2010000926

Acknowledgments
The author and publisher are grateful to the following for permission to reproduce copyright material: Alamy Images pp. **5** (© Richard Levine), **24** (© Betty LaRue); © Capstone Global Library p. **4** (John Millar); © Capstone Publishers pp. **8, 26, 27** (Karon Dubke); Corbis p. **10** (David Zimmerman); Getty Images p. **12** (Bongarts/Gunnar Berning); istockphoto p. **18** (© Elena Moiseeva); Photolibrary pp. **14 right, 25** (Gunnar Kullenberg); shutterstock pp. **14 left** (© Michele Perbellini), **16** (© Marek Slusarczyk), **22** (© JCEIv).

Photographs used to create silhouettes: istockphoto, Italy (©John Woodcock); shutterstock, Great Britain (©Alfonso de Tomas), Pisa (© Oleg Babich), United States (© Dr_Flash).

Cover photograph of a road winding through wilderness reproduced with permission of Photolibrary (Ingram Publishing).

Every effort has been made to contact copyright holders of material reproduced in this book. Any omissions will be rectified in subsequent printings if notice is given to the publisher.

Disclaimer
All the Internet addresses (URLs) given in this book were valid at the time of going to press. However, due to the dynamic nature of the Internet, some addresses may have changed or ceased to exist since publication. While the author and publisher regret any inconvenience this may cause readers, no responsibility for any such changes can be accepted by either the author or the publisher.

Contents

Words appearing in the text in bold, **like this,**
are explained in the glossary.

Measuring Distance

Distance is how far it is from one place or thing to another. If something is near to you, you can reach it quickly. If something is far from you, you have to travel farther to get to it.

When things are far in the distance, they look smaller than they really are close up.

We can use a yardstick, tape measure, or measuring wheel to measure distances. We use inches (in.) to measure very short distances. Longer distances are measured in feet (ft.) or sometimes yards (yd.), and very long distances in miles.

As you move a measuring wheel along, the distance is shown on the handle on a digital dial.

Distances on Maps

A map is a picture that shows an area shrunk down. A map can show a small area, such as your street. A map can also show a larger area, such as a country.

Earth is shaped like a ball, but this flat map makes it easy to look at the whole world at once.

ARCTIC OCEAN

North America

Europe

Asia

ATLANTIC OCEAN

PACIFIC OCEAN

Africa

PACIFIC OCEAN

South America

INDIAN OCEAN

Australia

SOUTHERN OCEAN

0   1500   3000 Miles
0   1500   3000 Kilometers

Antarctica

On many maps, every inch stands for a certain number of feet or miles on the ground. So we can measure a distance on the map and figure out how far that distance is in real life.

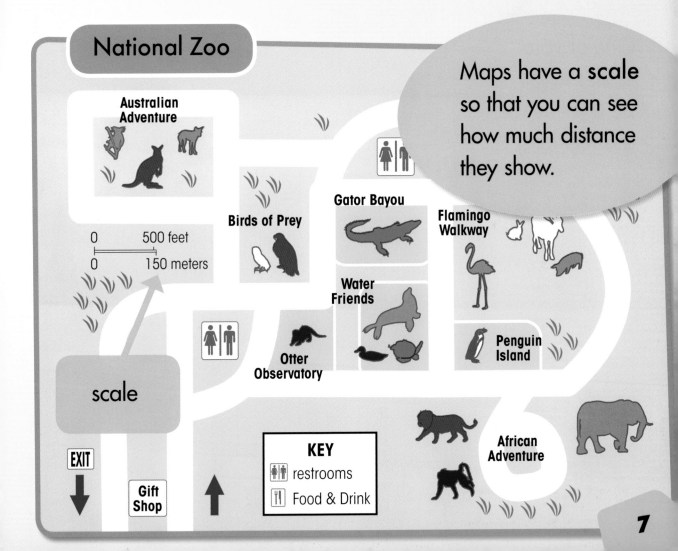

Maps have a **scale** so that you can see how much distance they show.

How Far Is One Stride?

Have you ever measured how far you can go in one **stride**? Compared to a younger brother or sister, you can go very far. But how far is far?

One of your strides might be a little under 2¼ feet long.

1 stride

The family room in your house might be about 20 feet wide. If you walked from one end of the room to the other, it would take about 9 strides.

1 living room

9 strides

What is farther than walking across your living room?

9

Down a Street

Streets can be long or short. When you walk down a street, you see other streets coming off from the sides. A **block** is the distance from one side street to the next one.

This photo of blocks in New York City was taken from a helicopter.

block

Blocks can be different lengths, but many blocks in New York City are about 264 feet long. This is a little more than 13 living rooms laid end to end.

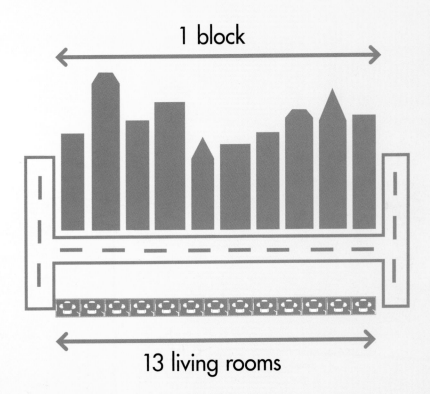

1 block

13 living rooms

What is farther than a walk down a city street? ➡

Along a Soccer Field

One end of a soccer field is far from the other. Soccer fields can be different sizes. The fields used for **international** matches must all be the same size.

Watching two countries play each other can be very exciting.

An international soccer field is 344 feet, or 155 yards, long. That is longer than a typical **block** in New York City.

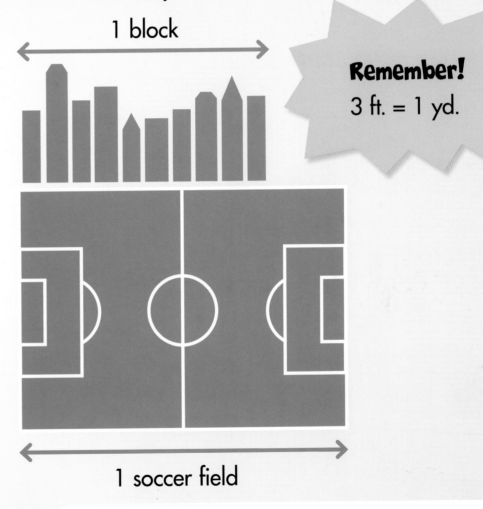

1 block

Remember!
3 ft. = 1 yd.

1 soccer field

What is farther than walking along a soccer field? ➡

Between Two Cities

Traveling from one city to another is much farther than walking along a soccer field. Distances this large are measured in miles.

Pisa

Florence

Pisa and Florence are two cities in Italy. The distance between Pisa and Florence is 43 miles. It would take almost an hour to drive from one to the other.

Italy

Remember!
1 mile = 5,280 ft.

Pisa

Florence

What can be farther than traveling from one city to the next? ➡

Along a Mountain Range

To go farther than from one city to the next, you could travel from one end of a **mountain range** to another. The Pyrenees are a fairly small mountain range in Europe.

Some parts of the Pyrenees are very snowy. Other parts are covered with thick forest.

The Pyrenees stretch about 267 miles from end to end. You would have to travel between Pisa and Florence more than six times to go as far as this.

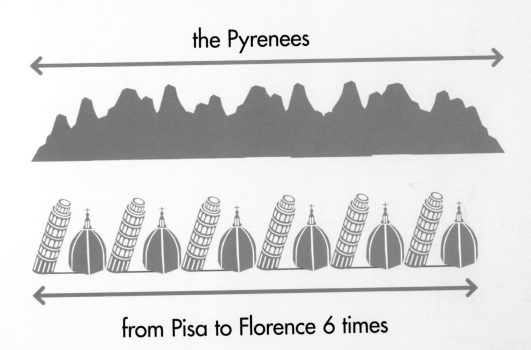

the Pyrenees

from Pisa to Florence 6 times

What can be farther than traveling the length of a mountain range? ➡️

The Length of Great Britain

The distance from one end of the island of Great Britain to the other is longer than the Pyrenees. The distance is often measured from a village in the north called John O'Groats, to the tip of the country in the southwest, called Land's End.

This signpost is at Land's End. It shows how many miles there are to John O'Groats if you travel by road.

If you went in a straight line, the distance from John O'Groats to Land's End is 602 miles. This is more than twice the length of the Pyrenees **mountain range**.

John O'Groats

the length of Great Britain

Land's End

2 lengths of the Pyrenees

What is farther than traveling the length of Great Britain? ➡

The Ganges River

The Ganges is a mighty river that flows through the countries of India and Bangladesh. If you traveled the length of the Ganges River, you would have gone much farther than the length of Great Britain.

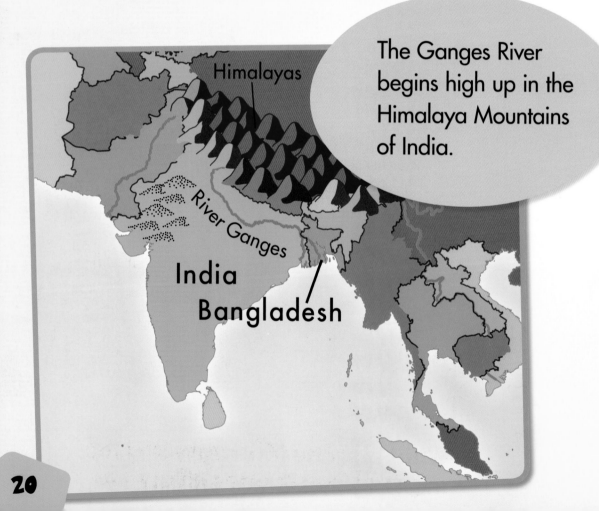

The Ganges River begins high up in the Himalaya Mountains of India.

Himalayas

River Ganges

India

Bangladesh

The Ganges River is 1,560 miles long, from its **source** to where it flows out into the sea. This is more than twice as far as the length of Great Britain. It is easier to see this if you show the river as a straight line.

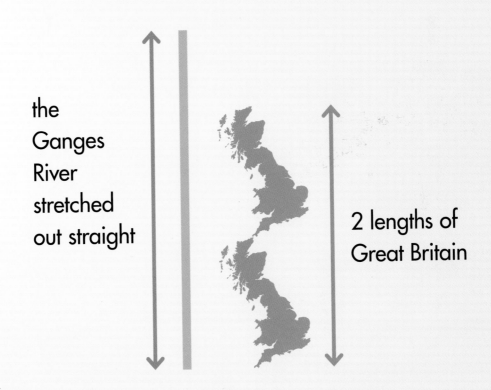

the Ganges River stretched out straight

2 lengths of Great Britain

What is farther than traveling the length of the Ganges River? ➡

Across the United States

Seattle and Miami are two cities on either side of the United States. Seattle is in the state of Washington, on the west coast. Miami is in the state of Florida, on the east coast.

Seattle

This photograph of the United States was taken from space.

Miami

Seattle and Miami are 2,727 miles apart. If you traveled the length of the Ganges River one and a half times, the distance between Seattle and Miami would still be farther.

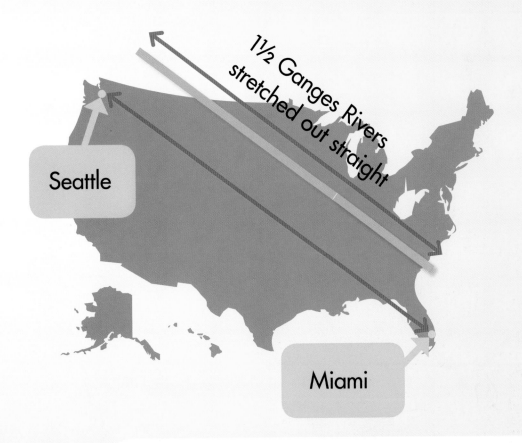

1½ Ganges Rivers stretched out straight

Seattle

Miami

What is farther than traveling across the United States?

Around the World

The **equator** is an imaginary line that goes all the way around the middle of the world. If you traveled around the equator once, you would go the enormous distance of 24,901 miles.

The equator crosses oceans and many different countries.

equator

The equator is more than nine times as long as the distance from Seattle to Miami. In fact, it is as far as you can go in a straight line—unless you head upward, into space!

Traveling around the world takes a long time. Most airplanes have to stop to **refuel** several times.

Measuring Activity

Things you will need: a yardstick, a tape measure, a pencil, and paper.

1. Take a big **stride** and ask a helper to measure how far you stepped, in feet. Write this down so you don't forget.

(2) Stride across the longest room in your house and count how many strides it takes. Again, write your answer down.

(3) Use the length of your stride to **estimate** how far you have walked in feet.

(4) Check your answer by measuring with a tape measure. How close was your estimate?

Distance Quiz and Facts

Very short distances are measured in inches (in.).
Larger distances are measured in feet (ft.) or yards (yd.).
Very large distances are measured in miles.

Quiz

1. What unit would you use to measure how far it is from one end of your country to the other?
   a) inches b) feet c) miles

2. What unit would you use to measure how far a coin can go with one push?
   a) inches b) feet c) miles

3. What unit would you use to measure how far it is from one end of your bedroom to the other?
   a) inches b) feet c) miles

Answers: 1 = c 2 = a 3 = b

> **Remember**
>
> 12 inches (in.) = 1 foot (ft.)
> 3 feet (ft.) = 1 yard (yd.)
> 5,280 feet (ft.) = 1 mile

Far Facts

- To travel the length of the Nile River, you would cover a distance of 4,132 miles. The Nile River is the longest river in the world.

- To travel the length of the Great Wall of China, you would cover a distance of 5,500 miles.

- If you could travel from the center of Earth to the center of the Moon, you would cover a distance of 238,854 miles.

- If you could travel from the center of Earth to the center of the Sun, you would cover a distance of almost 93 million miles.

Glossary

block distance from one street to the next

digital dial screen that shows numbers

equator imaginary line that runs around the middle of Earth, halfway between the North Pole and the South Pole

estimate to use what you know to make a good guess about something's size, amount, or value without measuring it

international involving two or more countries

mountain range group of mountains

refuel vehicles need fuel to make them move. When the fuel is nearly or all used up, more fuel must be added. This is refueling.

scale feature on a map that can be used to measure distance. A scale can show how many feet or miles on the ground are shown by each inch on the map.

source place where a river begins

stride big, deliberate step

Find Out More

Books

Block, Daniel R., and Marta Segal Block. *Reading Maps.* (*First Guide to Maps series*). Chicago: Heinemann Library, 2008.

Chancellor, Deborah. *Maps and Mapping.* Boston: Kingfisher, 2007.

Ritchie, Scot. *Follow That Map!: A First Book of Mapping Skills.* Toronto: Kids Can, 2009.

Web Sites

www.freemaptools.com/how-far-is-it-between.htm
Measure the distance between any two cities.

http://atlantis.coe.uh.edu/archive/science/science_lessons/scienceles3/length/length.html
Learn more about the history of measurement as well as other facts about units of length.

Index